AN UNOFFICIAL JOKE BOOK FOR FORTNITERS

SIDESPLITTING JOKES AND SHENANIGANS FROM SALTY SPRINGS

BRIAN BOONE

ILLUSTRATED BY AMANDA BRACK

Sky Pony Press
New York

Copyright © 2019 by Hollan Publishing, Inc.

Fortnite® is a registered trademark of Epic Games, Inc.

The Fortnite game is copyright © Epic Games, Inc.

All rights reserved. No part of this book may be reproduced in any manner without the express written consent of the publisher, except in the case of brief excerpts in critical reviews or articles. All inquiries should be addressed to Sky Pony Press, 307 West 36th Street, 11th Floor, New York, NY 10018.

Sky Pony Press books may be purchased in bulk at special discounts for sales promotion, corporate gifts, fund-raising, or educational purposes. Special editions can also be created to specifications. For details, contact the Special Sales Department, Sky Pony Press, 307 West 36th Street, 11th Floor, New York, NY 10018 or info@skyhorsepublishing.com.

Sky Pony® is a registered trademark of Skyhorse Publishing, Inc.®, a Delaware corporation.

Visit our website at www.skyponypress.com.

10 9 8 7 6 5

Library of Congress Cataloging-in-Publication Data is available on file.

Cover and interior illustrations by Amanda Brack
Cover design by Brian Peterson

Paperback ISBN: 978-1-5107-4807-1
E-book ISBN: 978-1-5107-4808-8

Printed in the United States of America

CONTENTS

INTRODUCTION

Has there ever been a game that captured the world's attention as quickly as Fortnite did? Gamers grabbed their controllers and phones as quickly as a Hero grabs loot out of an abandoned building on a Storm-ravaged island. (Sorry, we're *really* into Fortnite, too!)

Why wouldn't Fortnite be that popular? It's got all the thrills and spills of a first-person shooter, the build-it-yourself sky's-the-limit creativity of a sandbox game, plus an almost infinite cast of characters that includes everything from soldiers to ninjas to sharks to "mist monsters" to people in bear suits. Fortnite has a little something for everyone…plus dancing!

So "where are we landing" with this? The answer is *The Unofficial Joke Book for Fortniters*. There's a lot of loony loot in here, packed tighter than a chest and loaded up and ready to go like an SMG. You and your squad (even noobs!) will do the latest emote — The Laugh — when you pop out of the bush and peep these hilarious bits about the immersive world of Fortnite. We've got mats to delight and heal on every aspect of the game, including characters, weapons, locations, items, skins and more. You'll be a "Hero," you'll be "Epic," you'll be "Legendary" — no V-bucks required!

CHAPTER 1
THE SKIN YOU'RE IN

All about the characters that make Fortnite so special.

How do you heal a Tomato Head?
With tomato paste.

What's red and goes splat?
Tomato Head navigating a landing poorly.

What did Tony the Tomato do when he fell behind his teammates?
He had to ketchup.

Raider Rabbit really hates it when you sneak up on him.
It bugs Bunny!

What did the Fortnite skin do when he lost his cool mask?
He ran all the way Hime.

What Fortnite character would be great at soccer?
Striker!

I finally won a game as Trog.
It was quite a big feet!

Who's got the sickest beats and dopest rhymes in Fortnite?

Rap-tor.

•

How do Fortniters like fried chicken?

With extra skins!

•

I was going to play as a character other than the Cuddle Team Leader, but I couldn't bear it.

•

What do Fortniters eat for breakfast?

Flapjackies.

•

How do they eat them?

Off a Reinforced Backplate.

•

How does Ludwig cut loose?

He Lud-wigs out!

What does the pancake-loving Fortnite character wear on her feet?
Flip-Flop-Flapjackies.

Did you hear about the awkward Fortniter?
She was uncomfortable in her skin.

How come Cobalt skipped the Battle Royale?
He was feeling blue.

I tried using that cowgirl character but it was a real Calamity.

What should you say when you see Chomp Sr.?
"Looking sharp!"

Where would you find the Flytrap character?
Venus!

Why play Tricera Ops?
Because she's Tricera Tops!

•

Did you hear about that uncommon pickaxe?
Sure, what am I, an Armature?

•

Why do they call him Blue Striker?
Because if he was yellow they'd call him Yellow Striker.

•

Where on the island could you find Far Out Man?
Like, far out, man.

•

Which character has the best hair?
Lud-wig.

•

I've just got to get that skin, but I don't have enough
V-bucks. Help me, it's Desperado!

What skin smells like fish?
The Field Sturgeon.

Did you hear Chopper isn't going to be in the new season?
She got cut.

Play as Omega? That's the last thing I would do.

Why'd they make a character called Tomato Head?
Because if they made Mr. Potato Head they'd get sued!

One time I had Lynx to use and I didn't, and lost big. What a cat-astrophe!

●

Did you hear about the Fortnite player who got distracted and didn't get the chest full of back bling?
He was Bamboozled.

●

Who do you call to patch up a burned-out field?
A Field Surgeon.

●

What old animated movie do Fortniters like?
The Little Moisty Merman.

●

Which Hero has the least amount of money on him?
Cent-urion.

●

Did you hear about the hero with a tummy ache?
It was a gullet storm in Bullet Storm.

What should you do when your character loses Battle Royale?

Soldier on!

●

What happened when a Constructor met Demolisher?

They canceled each other out!

●

Looks like Nibbles is getting too old for this combat.

Look at his gray hare!

How do you offer a beverage to a dinosaur in Fortnite?
"Tea, Rex?"

•

How does Castor cast a spell?
"Llamacadabra!"

•

If you want to hear stories about other Fortnite battles, talk to Scaley.
He's got quite the tail.

•

What do you call it when Chomp is the last player standing?
Lone shark!

•

Whom does Chomp dress up as on Christmas?
Santa Jaws!

What do you call a cowardly hero?
Afraider.

●

What do you call it when Skirmisher gets a sword?
Cloak and dagger!

●

Did you hear Skirmisher finished off an opponent with just one weapon?
The stars were aligned!

●

What do you call it when a Ninja has no energy left?
A Shrunken Master.

●

What Outlander is great at chess?
Rook!

●

What's in Beef Boss's nose?
Durrrr boogers.

I got taken down by someone Legendary.
I guess it was Fate!

When can frostbite be deadly?
When it's Frostbite.

When is a storm not weather related?
When it's Bullet Storm.

What do you get when you cross Black Cat and Berserker?
Purrsserker!

How do you get Demolisher looking new?
With Demolisher polisher.

Why is playing with Lynx a great idea?
Because cats have nine lives!

Which character has the most badges?
Scout!

What's a Constructor's favorite movie?
Guardians of the Galaxy.

•

Drift's cat mask is the worst skin ever!
Nah, just kitten.

Why doesn't Castor go to school anymore?
He was ex-spelled.

•

Where do Tender Defenders come from?
Hatchbacks!

•

Ever use grab the Hatchback skin?
It's egg-cellent!

•

How does Santa get to his Fortnite game?
With his eight flying Raiders.

•

What's Spooky Team Leader's favorite childhood game?
Panda-Cakes.

•

What old song is definitely about Fortnite?
"Today is the day the TEDDY Bears have their picnic."

Are Spooky Team Leader and Fireworks Team Leader friends?

Bearly!

•

Did you know the Spooky Team Leader was actually behind the destructive Storm?

It was a Panda-demic.

•

Did you hear about how the Spooky Team Leader got spooked?

Someone screamed "Bam-BOO!"

•

Did you ever notice that the Cuddle Team Leader doesn't wear shoes?

It prefers to go barefoot.

•

Nibbles got burned up in a fight and he's all angry about it.

Talk about a hot, cross bun.

Do Fortniters gorge themselves?
No, they prefer Nibbles.

•

Cuddle Team Leader: You're looking beary nice today
Fireworks Team Leader: You've made me blush!
Cuddle Team Leader: Better just grin and bear it!

•

What's DJ Yonder's preferred item?
A Boombox!

•

Why do Tomato Heads fight at Durrr Burger?
There was beef between them.

•

What's a hungry Gnome's favorite place to eat?
Nom Noms!

•

How does the Moisty Merman head into battle?
With an octobus.

How does the Moisty Merman call his friends?
With a shell phone.

How do I get that Cat Lady skin?
I'll send you some Lynx.

Who's the best character for shelling?
Armadillo.

What would be a better name for Armadillo?
Mi-Shell.

What's pink or black and knows how much you weigh?
Scales.

Who guards the battle bus?
The Vanguard!

Who can see you even if you can't see her?
Eagle Eye.

•

Did you know that if you win a match as Tank Penny you
could have an extra life the next time you play as her? A
Penny saved is a Penny earned.

•

What game do Fortniters play before they land?
Mako Polo!

•

What Fortnite pet weighs the most?
Scales!

•

What food heals the Ice King?
Chilly.

Where did the Hero go after the explosion?
Everywhere!

•

Where did Rabbit Raider learn to fight?
In the Hare Force.

•

Did you hear about the new Pirate skin?
All he can use is the AR.

•

What's cute and dangerous?
Hamirez with a Submachine Gun!

•

I always play as Chomp Sr.
He's very so-fish-ticated.

•

What do Fortniters do at Christmas?
They make Mini Marauder houses!

What's the difference between a fruit with a mustache and Alpine Ace?

One's a Banana and the other wears a bandana.

•

What's the difference between a chicken man and blowing yourself up?

One's a Tender Defender and the other's a certain game-ender.

•

A Battle Royale came down to Rabbit Raider and Bunny Brawler. It was truly a race to the finish between the fast and the furriest.

•

Bunny Brawler was so upset she didn't win.

In fact, she was hopping mad!

•

Rabbit Raider wasn't available to play for a while last summer.

He got married and went on his bunnymoon.

What would really help Leviathan heal damage?
Some Vitamin Sea.

•

Why didn't Leviathan share his loot?
He's a little shellfish.

•

Did you hear that Leviathan traded in some weapons for V-bucks?
He went to a prawn shop.

•

Was Leviathan a terrible student?
Well, he never got anything above a Sea.

•

Did you hear that there was a fight in an old seafood restaurant on the island?
Everyone was battered.

•

The problem with Fortnite is that sometimes it's only skin deep.

What Fortnite skin could handle a volcano?
Magmus!

•

What Fortnite character could drive everyone into battle?
Magbus!

•

Is Krampus a good fighter to use?
Not really, he gets a lot of leg kramps.

•

Remember: pandas are rare, but PANDA Team Leaders are Legendary!

•

What Fortnite skin is the most educated?
Well-Read Knight.

•

What epic skin can bring you a sandwich?
Sub Commander!

Slushy Soldier was so honored to fight alongside the Spooky Team Leader. He absolutely melted!

What's Jack Gourdon's favorite of year?
Halloween. He really lights up!

Ever play as Galaxy?
It's out of this world!

Did you know you can outfit a donkey skin with a motor and turn it into a motorcycle?
Yep, it's a Yam-Yee-Haw.

What do you get when you cross a donkey skin with an Advanced Forces skin?
Yee-Hawk!

What do you call a Yee-Haw that's missing a leg?
A wonky donkey.

•

I hate playing as Beef Boss.
What a meathead!

•

Did you hear that Woofs accidentally exploded a building?
Talk about housebroken!

•

How are Woofs and the Wailing Woods similar?
Plenty of bark!

•

What's Yee-Haw's favorite video game?
Donkey Kong.

Did you hear that the Ice King adopted a Woofs?
Now he's a pup-sicle.

What is TEDDY short for anyway?
Theodore!

Why do they call him Chomp Sr.?
Because this is his last year of high school.

Mak Mari could've used a more effective weapon than smoke bombs.

It just seems kind of Dim.

•

What's a bunny skin's favorite football team?

The Oakland Rabbit Raiders.

•

Did you know that Woofs collects artifacts from the island before the storm?

He's a bark-e-ologist!

•

Who plays percussion in the Fortnite band?

Flappy Flyer — he's got drumsticks already.

•

What kind of birthday cake does Flappy Flyer prefer?

Coop-cakes!

Did you hear Flappy Flyer left an egg on Polar Peak?
Then it turned into an eggroll…

What's the worst part about being Fireworks Team Leader?
You can bearly breathe in that mask!

Did you hear that Spooky Team Leader threw a huge party?
It was a spooktacular!

Where does the Grill Sergeant eat dinner?
Sizzler.

What happens when you place on a Coven Cape on an uncommon skin character?
You get a Super Trooper!

CHAPTER 2
POINTS OF INTEREST

What's the most important thing in Fortnite? Location, location, location.

What item can freshen your breath in Fortnite?
Encamp-mints.

What happens when your player pulls a muscle in battle?
They get an en-cramp-ment.

Where did Tony Tomato disappear to?
Try Durrr Burger!

How is going to the Lonely Lodge like going fishing?
One has a scouting perch and the other is about scouting perch.

Where would you find giant sea creatures?
Whaling Woods.

Where would you find beautiful wild birds?
Pheasant Park.

Why did the player hide his chest in Farmland?
He was playing Crops and Robbers.

What's the dirtiest landing spot?
Dusty Depot.

What do you call a ninja at Retail Row?
The Maller Brawler.

●

How to play Fortnite: First you ride, then you glide, then you
decide the best place to hide!

●

I joined the Battle Bus with my new dentist character at the last minute.
I got in by the skin of my teeth!

●

What site is the biggest relief to land on?
Flush Factory.

●

Where can you send off messages and packages?
Mailing Woods.

●

I'd drop on Snobby Shore, but I'm just too good for that.

Where's the one place you don't want to find yourself on Valentine's Day?

The Lonely Lodge.

What's the most embarrassing place to land?

Blush Factory.

What's the loudest, most obnoxious place in Fortnite?

The Prattle Bus.

Where can you go to grab some cash?
Loan-ly Lodge.

•

Where do you not want to land?
Shock Tower.

•

Where can you find the best snacks in Fortnite?
At Salty Springs.

•

Where do cats like to wander in Fortnite?
At Purr Burger.

•

What's the most dangerous place to fish?
Risky Reels.

•

What's the slipperiest place to go?
Risky Peels.

What do you call someone who loots a Durrr Burger?
A Durrr Burger Burglar.

What's the easiest pass to navigate in Fortnite?
Battle Pass!

What's so great about Durrr Burger?
It's the only place where you can find guns *and* buns.

●

What's the luckiest place to land?
Lucky Landing!

●

Where can you find some of the best outfits for your Fortnite players?
In the Outskirts.

●

Where does Krampus sleep?
At an en-kramp-ment.

●

Where's the best place to play golf in Fortnite?
Lazy Links!

●

Fortnite is about the only time in life when you *want* to go to a prison!

Where on the map can you find the best ice cream?
At Frosty Flights.

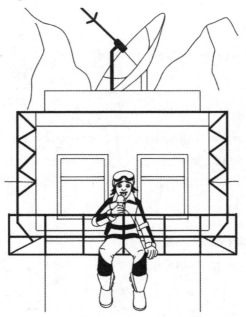

What song is always playing in Frosty Flights?
"Winter Wonderland."

What's the most odious place to land?
Peasant Park.

What kind of bush would you find in Shifty Shafts?
Ambush!

I hate playing in Moisty Mire. I always get "bogged" down
there.

What's the biggest mission in Fortnite?
Transmission Towers.

●

How do mushrooms grow in Snobby Shores?
With snobby spores!

●

Did you hear they changed the name of Leaky Lake to Loot
Lake? It just leaked out.

●

Where can you buy gifts on the island?
Present Park.

●

What buildings should have been a lot taller?
Stilted Towers.

●

What landing spot never works out?
Faulty Springs.

Where should you go for new footwear?
Boot Lake.

•

Where do you find Paradise Palms?
At the ends of Paradise Arms.

•

How should you dress for a trip to Pleasant Park?
A pleasant parka.

•

How does your mouth feel after a Durrrr Burger?
Like a Greasy Grove.

•

Where would you find terrible flowers?
Wilted Towers.

CHAPTER 3
THE GUN SHOW

This chapter is packing all kinds of firepower.

Have you played Fortnite?
It's the bomb!

•

How do Fortniters order their coffee drinks?
With a double pump (of anything).

•

How do Fortniters like their eggs?
Scrambler!

•

What's a Fortniter's nose filled with?
Bogeys.

How do you make a Fortniter dance?
Drop a boogie bomb.

How do you make a Fortniter pick their nose?
Drop a boogie bomb.

WHISPER .45: I'm so sad.
PLAYER: Hey, cheer up. Don't be so suppressed!

How do you see better in Fortnite?
Wear your Googlys!

•

What's the best place to find Fortnite tips?
Just Googly them!

•

How do you feed a big gun in Fortnite?
Grab it a sub sandwich.

•

What kind of weapon smells minty-fresh?
A Scoped assault rifle.

•

I found some Hop Rocks, but I was kind of disappointed.
I wanted something a little meteor.

•

What Fortnite weapon works best underwater?
A sub-machine gun.

What kind of weapon is full of ice cream?
A scooped assault rifle.

●

What kind of assault rifle can you drive?
A SCAR!

●

**Did you hear about the Fortnite player who replaced his
friend's SMG with another gun?**
It was a tactical joke.

●

Did you hear about the assault rifle that exploded?
It was a burst!

●

**What's the difference between an assault rifle and a new
driver?**
One's an M16 and the other is 16.

What happens when you cross a pig with a special pistol?
You get a ham cannon.

What happens if you put too many bullets in a pump shotgun?
You get a plump shotgun.

Where should you keep a treasure?
Close to the chest.

What's a Fortniter's favorite kind of hip hop?
Trap.

Where do Fortniters put their cups?
On Flying Saucers.

What kind of stone will you find 99 of during a game of Battle Royale?
Tombstones.

Why couldn't the Hero lift his treasure?
He had chest pains.

What should you say if you want to borrow a friend's gun?
"AR you gonna use that?"

Why did the SCAR only shoot plastic darts?
Because it got nerfed.

What weapon shoots trivia instead of bullets?
A Factical Shotgun!

What's a better term for "getting blown up by a grenade?"
Saluting the frag.

It's so hard to decide what melee weapon to use.
It's positively wrenching!

What do you feed a sword?
Slice cream.

What did one sword say to other sword?
"You're looking sharp!"

How do Fortniters send letters?
With an axe machine.

How do you select the perfect Fortnite weapon?
Find something you like; just rifle through.

What do melee fighters smell like?
Axe Body Spray.

●

What did the well-armed melee fighter say at the end of the game?
Bats all, folks!

●

How do Fortniters have fun in the winter?
They go rocket sledging.

●

Why did the Hero win a debate with a Diamond Sword?
He had a good point.

●

Why's it called the Infinity Blade?
Because you'll look for it for infinity!

●

What do you call a big weapon that destroys buildings?
A heavy sniper.

What do you call a smashed SMG?
A Compact SMG.

●

What do you call a bed that fits the whole squad?
A Quadcrasher.

●

Want to be good at Fortnite?
AIM high!

●

What's the best Easter egg in Fortnite?
Eggshell — it's literally an Easter egg!

●

Why couldn't the special chute deploy?
It wasn't up to the Tusk.

●

What's round and never makes a sound?
Rescue Ring.

What tool could you wear on your head?
A turbine.

●

Better name for a mini-gun: an assault trifle.

●

What do you call damage you endure right when you start playing?
Storm drain.

●

What's a Fortniter's favorite fast food place?
ARby's

●

What medical supplies bounce right off a wound?
Rubber bands!

●

How do you get to sit at the front of the Battle Bus?
Yell, "shotgun!"

What kind of weapon will attack your opponents with custard and jam?

An assault trifle.

●

How can you tell that pirates like Fortnite?

They're into loot.

What happens when you mix Tomato Head with a flamethrower?

Hot salsa!

Fortnite saying: An apple a day . . . means you won't be in the game for long.

●

I got this weapon out of the garbage, and it doesn't even work. That's the last time I use a Dump Shotgun.

●

How do you ruin a birthday party in Fortnite?
Blow up the balloons . . . with a Clinger.

●

What do you call two players with Clingers?
A blast-off.

●

What should you get from a Clinger?
As far away as possible.

●

What does a Valentine from a Clinger say?
"I'm stuck on you!"

What's the tastiest candy in Fortnite?
Supply drops!

•

What do you call it when the Fireworks Team Leader finds a can of food?
A Meeet Cute!

•

How long does it take for a Small Shield Potion to work?
A weak!

•

What kind of player does a mushroom heal the most quickly?
One who's a fungi!

•

Did you hear about the birthday party on the island?
It was a blowout!

•

What pioneer discovered the island's troves of weapons?
Daniel Boom.

What makes an apple in Fortnite so special?
It's a meal and a heal!

●

Why did the Fortniter play two games at the same time?
He wanted double the Bubble!

●

What are the least destructive guns in Fortnite?
Finger guns.

What are the best battle wounds in Fortnite?
SCARs!

What's a Fortniter's favorite part of a concert?
The bands.

•

What's a Fortniter's favorite candy?
Hop Rocks.

•

Hop Rocks are so unreliable.
They could never understand the gravity of the situation.

•

How did the Hop Rock's parents punish it?
They grounded it!

•

I always like to carry plenty of bullets of various sizes.
What can I say? It's my M.O.

•

What weapon is best when it's cold outside?
A SCAR, of course. (Read it out loud.)

How does a Stink Bomb smell?
With its nose.

•

I collected every type of weapon there is. They were all in tiers!
I paid my Fortnite expert friend to play on my squad. You
    could say she was a hired gun.

•

**Did you hear about the Fortniter who wanted a Bitemark
    pickaxe?**
Her friends got it for her — they all chipped in!

•

Did you hear about the Fortnite player who won the Battle
    Royale at the last minute with a well-placed grenade?
    And that's what we call a zinger of a Clinger.

•

**If you can't find wall-making supplies, where can you
    buy them?**
Wall-Mart!

Did you hear about the Hero who kept dropping her pistol?
Talk about a loose cannon!

•

There are a lot of Fortnite weapons you can't use right now.
Hey, it's nobody's vault.

•

Fortnite is about the only place where getting fired is a good
thing!

•

I found a great weapon right on the edge of the island. Talk
about a shore shot!

•

I didn't like it the first time I used that assault rifle. It was
kind of SCAR-y!

•

I was going to use some sniper rifles until another player
shot it down.

What do you call a shotgun with a knot in it?
An impractical shotgun.

•

What's the difference between a Hero and a great weapon?
One's buff and one's buffed!

•

What weapon can take down a tree?
A stump-action shotgun.

•

What weapon shoots Thanksgiving turkeys?
A plump-action shotgun.

•

What happened to the sneaky sniper?
He bolted!

•

What's an assault rifle's favorite candy?
SCAR-Burst.

How do you make a Battle Bus float?
Put it in a glass of root beer.

•

When's a good time to use your Black Shield?
When your White Shield is in the shop.

•

Where do the best Fortnite builders study their craft?
At Prince-Stone.

•

What do Fortnite builders eat in the late afternoon?
Tea and stones.

•

Why would Superman be a great Fortnite builder?
He's the Man of Steel!

•

How are Fortnite characters so strong?
They all pump iron.

How do Fortnite characters keep their clothes so crisp?
The game is full of irons.

•

What old song do Fortnite builders like to emote to?
"Brick House."

•

Why build a wall?
It helps if you're on the brick of disaster!

•

Why did the angry Hero grab a weak weapon?
She had an axe to grind.

•

What happens if you drink too many healing items too fast?
You get potion sickness.

•

What's another name for a legendary weapon?
Top gun!

What happens if you build in Fortnite for too long?
You'll go wall-eyed!

●

What did the Hero say when he lost his rifle?
"Hey, where's my rifle?"

●

Why did the Hero look over his wall?
Because he couldn't see through it.

●

How does a Fortniter pick his nose?
With a pickaxe!

●

Some objects appear common and then you find out they're rare. It seems like there's a lot of gray area.

●

There's a Fortnite weapon so legendary . . . that it doesn't actually exist!

CHAPTER 4
SO EMOTE-TIONAL

If you feel like laughing at these jokes about emotes, you don't even have to wait to the end!

Fortniters sure love to emote.
I mean, who doesn't like to bogey and then boogie.

•

What would you find around a castle in Fortnite?
An e-moat.

•

Who does the Floss at Buckingham Palace?
The Royale Family!

•

Why do Fortnite players have beautiful teeth?
They never fail to Floss!

What kind of emote is also a treat at the county fair?
Candy Floss.

How do you make your TV do the Floss?
With your emote control!

•

What kind of music do wistful Fortniters enjoy?
Emo(te).

Why are Fortniters hard to have serious talks with?
They always dance around the issue.

•

What's a Fortniter's favorite reality show?
Emoting with the Stars.

•

What's the difference between the bush and an emote?
One's a grove and one's a groove.

•

What would a Fortniter call dancing at sea?
An emote in a boat!

•

Does the Battle Bus emote?
Sure, it can brake dance.

•

Where's the best place in California to emote?
San Frandisco.

What dance is Moonwalker's favorite?
The Moonwalk, of course!

Why can't Bonesy do any emotes?
Two left feet.

●

What emote does the Maki Monster like best?
The Maki Monster Mash.

A Fortnite player tried to kick his emote habit…but he wound up doing the Squat Kick instead.

•

What do Fortniters put on their toast?
Groove Jam.

•

What do Fortniters drink with their breakfast toast?
Orange Justice.

•

Did you hear about the Fortniter who got so sick of winning rounds? Yeah, he came down with a bad case of Disco Fever.

•

What's the one way besides the Battle Bus to get to the island?
Take the L!

I do my favorite emote at the end of every game: The Robot.
  It's almost as if it's… automatic.

What's the most dangerous thing about emotes?
You can fall into a groove!

●

When is it the appropriate time to do the T-Pose?
At T-Time!

What's the cleanest emote dance?
Tidy!

What's the best thing you can drop in Fortnite?
The Bass!

What snack goes great with emoting?
Dip!

Did you hear about the player who did an emote when he lost his pet?
He did the Bonesyless.

Did you hear that the Fortnite player was sad when they lost the game?
They immediately had to Cheer Up!

Truly there is no tastier emote than Treat Yourself!

What's a good name for a lady who loves to emote?
Dabra.

•

You don't have to emote that long, you know. A little Dab
  will do ya.

**What's a good name for a person who loves the Capoeira
  emote?**
Martial!

I finally got to do a Cat Flip the other day, and I'm proud to say it was purrfect. Absolutely un-fur-gettable.

•

After defeating 99 other players, you can do the Calculated emote if you like. Hey, the math checks out.

•

What's the one thing you've got to tidy up before an emote?
Brush Your Shoulders off!

•

That winning player just exploded into a dance.
She'd really reached her Breaking Point.

•

There was a Fortnite player who fell in love with another Fortnite player, and when she was done, she emoted with the Flippin' Incredible. I guess you could say she was head over heels!

•

I tried to do an emote…but I was Denied!

When I won Battle Royale the other day, I broke into a Backstroke. It went swimmingly!

Lots of people have picked up on the Baller emote. It's really going a-round.

What emote is so great is resonates for a long time?
"Echo"-lades!

What kind of emote can you do while still holding a weapon?
The Double Fist Pump.

I wanted to emote, but I didn't have a moment. Things were in Flux.

How do you keep your guns into the emote phase?
When you do the Gun Show!

Why did the Fortniter always use the True Heart emote?
He just loved it!

•

What emote would you find in a chest?
True Heart!

•

Did you hear about the Fortniter who did the Sprinkler so
 well that it shorted out his phone?

•

Why didn't the Fortniter do the Lazy Shuffle?
She didn't feel like it.

•

Why did the Fortniter like the Jugglin' emote?
He had a lot of balls in the air.

•

When's the best time to Floss?
At tooth-hurty.

I'm great at Fortnite and my favorite emote is the Hitchhiker. What can I say, I'm all thumbs!

●

What do you do after an emote?
Fmote.

●

What's a Cube Monster's favorite emote?
Reanimated!

●

The Fortniter wanted to do the Pumpernickel, but didn't have the 500 V-Bucks. Just not enough bread.

●

The Fortniter wanted to know if his friends saw him do the On the Hook emote. He was just fishing for compliments!

●

I don't mean to box you in, but you're great at the Mime Time emote!

When's the one time in Fortnite when a storm is a celebration?

When you Make it Rain!

•

What's the Storm King's favorite emote?

Make it Reign!

•

What's a Fortniter's favorite non-video game?

Rock Paper Scissors!

CHAPTER 5
AAAAAAAAH!

All about those monsters from Mists, Cubes, and other places around the island one shouldn't explore too closely.

Where do Fortnite monsters shop for their clothes?
In the Husk-y section.

Who's the most attractive mist monster?
A Cute Zombie!

What's the biggest pageant in Fortnite?
Mist America.

You've got to feel for those Cube Monsters. All they want is a square meal.

AAAAAAAAH!

Where on the island will you find Cube Monsters?
In the town square!

●

Not only are they vicious, those Cube Monsters are nerds.
What a bunch of squares!

How is a Cube Monster like a math class?
The square roots.

If a Cube Monster could emote, what would it choose?
A square dance!

Will it hurt if a Mimic bites you?
Yes, to be totally toothful.

What do Smashers eat?
Smashed potatoes.

Did you hear about the Fortniter who got laser eye surgery?
He thought it would turn him into a Blaster.

What does a Beehive's wife call him?
Honey.

What Mist Monster is the most fearsome?
The Blaster. The eyes have it!

What did the Fortniter who got the Taker in the Secret Santa buy?

Nothing!

•

How can you tell if a Chicken Trooper took over the body of a Pitcher?

If he bocks.

•

What's the difference between a player at the beginning of a Fortnite round and a Husk?

One hides in the brambles, and the other one shambles.

•

What are rotten but not forgotten?

Husks.

•

Why don't Husks smell?

They're dead and their noses don't work.

A bunch of Husky Husks surround you while a Lobber launches screaming fire bombs at you. Who gets killed first?

You.

What's black and white and dead all over?

A Husk in a tuxedo.

Never follow a Husk. It's a dead end.

●

What would you find inside of a Husk?
Corn!

●

Did you hear they're getting rid of monsters in the next Fortnite season?
They won't be mist.

●

Why did the Husk cross the road?
To kill you.

●

What does a Beehive read?
Buzzfeed.

●

What's a Beehive's favorite weapon?
A Bee-Bee gun.

Lots of players love the Beehive.
There's a lot of buzz!

●

Where does a Husk go out for dinner?
Red Lobber.

●

How is a Pitcher different from a pitcher?
Every pitch is a wild pitch!

●

Pitchers are fearsome Husks. No bones about it!

●

How are Husks so persistent?
Dead-ication.

●

Should you try to blow up a 'Sploder's propane tank before he can?
Hey, it's worth a shot.

Never get into a conversation with a 'Sploder. It'll just blow
  up for no reason!

●

Never trust a Beehive. They're always bumbling around.

Never get into a conversation with a Husk. They just
  shamble on and on and on . . . .

Never talk to a Blaster. They'll really shoot you a look.

Flingers are always welcome at my parties. They've just got a glow about them.

Why couldn't the Taker get away?
Some things just don't fly.

What's the difference between Fortnite and a Mimic?
One runs on bytes and the other one bites.

How can you tell if a Beehive is nearby?
It suddenly gets very swarm.

Where do things go when Husks blow them up?
Kingdom Come!

Why do 'Sploders carry gas tanks?
Because they're pro-pain.

Why did the 'Sploder cross the road?
To blow up the people on the other side.

●

Can you name forty creatures from Fortnite?
39 Husky Husks and a 'Sploder.

Where do things go when Husks blow them up?
Kingdom Come!

•

I love encountering Flingers. What can I say? I'm hooked!

•

What happened to the man who tried to reform a Lobber?
The project blew up in his face.

•

What's blue and has four wheels?
A Chrome Husky. We were kidding about the wheels.

•

Why are Lobbers such worthy foes?
They act very skull-fully.

•

I was just playing a game as normal, and then boom, a Flinger showed up. It really threw me!

Takers weren't very popular at first . . . but then they just took off!

●

What happens if you give a Taker a root beer?
A root beer float!

●

Do Smashers carry V-bucks around?
No, they prefer to just charge.

●

What's a 'Sploder's favorite toy?
A BOOMerang.

●

What happens when you put ten 'Sploders into a room together?
An explosively good time.

●

What's a 'Sploder's favorite TV show?
The Big Bang Theory.

What award did a Zapper win in his high school yearbook?
Most Explosive.

MOST EXPLOSIVE

How do Husks remain so calm when they're attacking?
Because nothing gets under their skin!

•

Why don't Husks have many friends?
They have explosive tempers.

AAAAAAAAH!

Why was the Lobber full of regret?
Because she mis-threw her skull and it didn't hit anything.

•

Did you know there's a Cube Monster that loves to emote?
The Boogeyman!

•

How do you heal a Cube Monster?
With a Dead-Kit.

•

What will lead you to a Mist Monster's hideout?
Mist Monstairs!

•

Why is the Blaster such an effective Mist Monster?
Because of its laser-like focus!

•

What happens if you give healing fruit to a Beehive?
You get Applebees.

How can you find a Mimic?
Chest you wait, they'll let you know!

●

I used to hate Flingers, but now I like them. They're really glowing on me!

●

What would you get if you crossed a 'Sploder and a primate?
A ba-boom.

●

What do you call a Monster's odor?
A Husk musk.

●

Three Husks walk into a building. They wreck the place that took you hours to build.

●

A Husk goes into work. His boss asks, "Did you sleep last night? You look a little bit dead."

AAAAAAAAH!

What goes "Ha Ha BOOM"?
A 'Sploder who heard a good joke.

●

What kind of structures could Blasters build?
Laser beams!

●

What kind of dog would you never want to find in Fortnite?
A Husky!

●

Why does Fortnite have all these monsters anyway?
Husk because!

CHAPTER 6
SQUAD!

Some funny conversations you might hear over the headset.

PLAYER ONE: Do you want to hear a TEDDY joke?
PLAYER TWO: No, I couldn't bear it!

PLAYER ONE: Do you want to play the new Fortnite update?
PLAYER TWO: 'Tis the season!

PLAYER ONE: Do you want to play as Arachne?

PLAYER TWO: No thanks, I'm Arachne-phobic.

•

PLAYER ONE: Have you heard much about ELF?

PLAYER TWO: A little.

PLAYER ONE: Tony Tomato sure was in a bad mood today.
PLAYER TWO: Yeah, he was rather saucy.

•

PLAYER ONE: I'm going with Prodigy today.
PLAYER TWO: Seems really smart!

•

PLAYER ONE: Don't worry about that guy crouching down.
PLAYER TWO: Why not?
PLAYER ONE: He's bush league.

•

PLAYER ONE: Can I offer you some emotes?
PLAYER TWO: Oh, just a Dab.

•

PLAYER ONE: Which constructor is your favorite?
PLAYER TWO: I'd say it's Guardian . . . overall.

PLAYER ONE: Scales wasn't much help today.

PLAYER TWO: Yeah, he was really dragon.

PLAYER ONE: Cuddle Team Leader will guarantee you a win every time!

PLAYER TWO: That's a bear-faced lie!

●

PLAYER ONE: Who sent all these cows in to fight?

PLAYER TWO: Oh sorry, I thought you said Cattle Bus.

PLAYER ONE: Who sent in all these babies to fight?
PLAYER TWO: They thought it was the Rattle Bus.

•

PLAYER ONE: My friend only played Fortnite for half a month.
PLAYER TWO: That's too weak.

•

PLAYER ONE: I heard you had to walk away from your game and lost all your stats!
PLAYER TWO: It was an axe-ident!

•

PLAYER ONE: Want to drop on Snobby?
PLAYER TWO: Shore!

•

PLAYER ONE: I know it's epic, but I find that back bling at Oktoberfest every time I play.
PLAYER TWO: You do?
PLAYER ONE: Yep, Clockworks!

PLAYER ONE: Load up on guns!

PLAYER TWO: Why is your character's mouth blowing bubbles?

PLAYER ONE: Oh I thought you said load up on gums.

●

PLAYER ONE: Hey, get your character to eat these old burgers.

PLAYER TWO: No way!

PLAYER ONE: Come on, I Durrr you!

●

PLAYER ONE: Have you ever played as Double Agent?

PLAYER TWO: A couple of times.

●

PLAYER ONE: Am I too late to join the game?

PLAYER TWO: Not at all. Thanks for "dropping" in!

●

PLAYER ONE: Did you get Battlehawk?

PLAYER TWO: Yes, he came with the patch.

PLAYER ONE: I haven't played as Taro in a while, so I think I will.

PLAYER TWO: It's nice to get back to your roots.

•

PLAYER ONE: Don't ever worry about dropping your Woofs and not being able to get it back.

PLAYER TWO: Why not?

PLAYER ONE: It has collar ID.

•

PLAYER ONE: Hey, did you see that Ninja?

PLAYER TWO: No.

PLAYER ONE: Good!

•

PLAYER ONE: How many explosives do you have?

PLAYER TWO: C . . . 4.

PLAYER ONE: Yes but how many?

PLAYER TWO: C4!

PLAYER ONE: Nevermind.

PLAYER ONE: Want to visit Frosty Flights for a minute?
PLAYER TWO: Sure, I'll have a Polar Peak!

•

PLAYER ONE: I don't do emotes after a game.
PLAYER TWO: What are you, Chicken?

PLAYER ONE: Do you wanna have an emote fight?
PLAYER TWO: Bring It!

PLAYER ONE: Why do you always do the IDK?
PLAYER TWO: I dunno.

PLAYER ONE: I know you won, but you don't have to rub it in.
PLAYER TWO: Hey, I was showing Respect!

PLAYER ONE: You *really* found a huge field of apples?
PLAYER TWO: Yeah! It's the heal deal!

PLAYER ONE: Hey, who's on your squad?
PLAYER TWO: Aidan, Braden, Jaden…
PLAYER ONE: …and Hayden?
PLAYER TWO: No. And me!

PLAYER ONE: You ever heard of that special assault rifle?
PLAYER TWO: Of course I have. It's famas!

PLAYER ONE: Just you wait, I'm gonna win this Battle Royale and bust out an emote!

PLAYER TWO: Oh Snap!

PLAYER ONE: Yeah, that's the one.

PLAYER ONE: I spotted a rare weapon and then another player got to it before I could.

PLAYER TWO: Gosh, you really blue it!

PLAYER ONE: Are you happy with that ammo?
PLAYER TWO: You could say it . . . rocks!

•

PLAYER ONE: You want to borrow a rocket launcher?
PLAYER TWO: I'll give it a shot!

•

PLAYER ONE: Why did you use that Impulse Grenade?
PLAYER TWO: I just had the sudden urge to do it!

•

PLAYER ONE: Why did you build two sets of stairs?
PLAYER TWO: I wanted to have a staring contest.

•

PLAYER ONE: I've got some questions about weapons.
PLAYER TWO: Hey, you can always axe a question!

•

PLAYER ONE: I'm all out of ammo.
PLAYER TWO: The next round is on me!

CHAPTER 7
GOOD GAME!

Are you a Fortnite master...or a hopeless noob?

YOU KNOW YOU'RE A FORTNITER IF...

...You don't take a bath, you hide in an OP bathtub.

...When you take a bath, you always move toward the Bubbles.

...When you watch *Star Wars,* you root for the Storm Troopers.

...You don't call it a "medicine cabinet" you call in a med-kit.

...You're constantly craving Durrrr Burger burgers.

...When your coach tells you to take one shot...you run over and try to knock him ovcr.

...You changed your name to Gus.

…You open the refrigerator door slowly to make sure there isn't a Riot Husky behind there.

…You don't call it the school cafeteria, you call it the Lunchpad.

…You don't go to the bathroom, you drop at Flushing Fields.

…You call a florist "the Rose Team Leader."

…Your doctor says your metal levels are high and you think that's a good thing.

…You don't call it the bathroom, you call it a Flush Factory.

…Your dream car is a hatchback.

…You only drink from Chug-Jugs, never glasses.

…You store all your wealth in a treasure chest instead of a bank.

…You take your pizza with mushrooms and apples.

…You greet people with "Gimme some skin!"

…When you watch a football game, you wonder why everyone is wearing a Blitz skin.

…You make eggs with a pickaxe and cut wood with a Scrambler.

…You hate it when you get unwanted emails, or Meeet.

…You like your food Fiery.

…You don't go to school dances, but you would go to a school emote.

…You peel a banana and wonder where its mustache went.

…You always ask for extra tomatoes.

…Your favorite character in *The Wizard of Oz* is Hay Man.

…You try to cut with a lollipop and lick a pickaxe.

…You think *The Nutcracker* is about Crackshot e-moting.

…You don't say "yes," you say "Yee-Haw!"

…In science class, you thought it was called the Periodic Table of the Elementals.

…On the night before Christmas, visions of Sugarplum dance in your head.

…You get a little panicky on a misty morning.

…You see a broken-down car and wonder how much metal you could salvage out of it.

…You celebrate when whenever you spot a garden gnome in somebody's yard.

...You think Shakespeare could have really improved that one play if he'd called it *Happy Hamlet*.

...You don't wake up in the morning, you set your alarm clock to "res" you.

...You don't tell your parents that you improved your grade, you "buffed" it!

...You call your bedroom closet a hangar.

...You don't request a "table for four" you ask for a "quad launch."

...You've planted a protective wall around your home.

...You think of the American flag being red, trainee, and rare.

...You ride the "Battle Bus" to school.

...You ask your bus driver, "Where we landing?"

...You call the food court at the mall Greasy Grove.

…You call mandarin oranges "Little Legendaries."

…You're thinking about pursuing a career as a pirate, what with all the treasure chests.

…On cloud-free days, you comment on how the sky is looking "rare."

…You're not a redhead, you're a Ginger Gunner.

YOU'RE SO BAD AT FORTNITE THAT...

…When you jumped off the Battle Bus you landed on top of the Battle Bus.

…You scared off the Storm!

…You keep wondering when your player will build their little house out of blankets.

…The game made you stay on the Battle Bus.

…Whenever you sign in, Battle Royale is suddenly only for 99 players and it's full.

…A Port-A-Fort lasts longer than your player does.

…When other players say Something Stinks, they're not talking about the emote.

…You don't buy things at the store, you make an "in-game purchase."

…You somehow die on the Battle Bus.

…You grab a Submachine Gun and somehow your player drowns.

…You thought that *Solo* would be about the greatest Fortnite player ever.

…You thought that "AR" meant "Advanced Reader."

…You've never gotten to emote!

CHAPTER 8
KNOCKED!

Don't get knocked by these Fortnite knock-knock jokes.

Knock-Knock
Who's there?
Matt.
Matt who?
Want me to leave these Mats out there on the mat?

•

Knock-knock!
Who's there?
Lydia.
Lydia who?
Lydia chest looks a bit loose. Better fix it or all that good stuff will fall out.

Knock-knock!
Who's there?
Husk.
Husk who?
Husk me again!

Knock-knock!
Who's there?
Orange.
Orange who?
Orange you glad you're Legendary?

Knock-knock!
Who's there?
Barry.
Barry who?
Barry that chest before anyone can steal it!

Knock-knock!
Who's there?
Philip.
Philip who?
Philip my med-kit!

Knock-knock!
Who's there?
Alpaca.
Alpaca who?
Alpaca chest full of useful stuff!

Knock-knock!
Who's there?
Chest.
Chest who?
Chest got on the Battle Bus!

Knock-knock!
Who's there?
Chest?
Chest who?
Chest checking in!

Knock-knock!
Who's there?
AR.
AR who?
AR you in there?

Knock-knock!
Who's there?
AR.
AR who?
AR you gonna play Fortnite later?

Knock-knock!
Who's there?
Assault.
Assault who?
Assault and pepper for these eggs would be nice.

Knock-knock!
Who's there?
Mustache.
Mustache who?
I mustache you if you're gonna use your banana!

Knock-knock!
Who's there?
Hay.
Hay who?
Hay man!

Knock-knock!
Who's there?
Chute.
Chute who?
Oh chute, I thought I'd fly right in!

Knock-knock!
Who's there?
Gum.
Gum who?
Gumshoe!

Knock-knock!
Who's there?
Quinn.
Quinn who?
Quinn are you going to play Fortnite?

Knock-knock!
Who's there?
AC.
AC who?
AC you out there.

Knock-knock!
Who's there?
Buzz.
Buzz who?
Isn't knocking enough?

Knock-knock!
Who's there?
Jess.
Jess who?
Jess let me in already!

Knock-knock!
Who's there?
Specter.
Specter who?
Specter you to know who it was already.

Knock-knock!
Who's there?
Deadeye.
Deadeye who?
Deadeye do that?

Knock-knock!
Who's there?
Rook.
Rook who?
Rook who it is!

Knock-knock!
Who's there?
Gunner.
Gunner who?
Gunner let me in?

Knock-knock!
Who's there?
Flash.
Flash who?
Gesundheit!

Knock-knock!
Who's there?
Rush.
Rush who?
Bless you!

Knock-knock!
Who's there?
Commando.
Commando who?
I didn't know you can yodel.

Knock-knock!
Who's there?
Nog Ops.
Nog Ops who?
Nog Ops to no good I bet!

Knock-knock!
Who's there?
Chopper.
Chopper who?
Chopper 'til you drop!

Knock-knock!
Who's there?
Maven.
Maven who?
Maven you want to team up?

Knock-knock!
Who's there?
Triple Threat.
Triple Threat who?
Hello hello hello!

Knock-knock!
Who's there?
Galaxy.
Galaxy who?
Galaxy later I guess.

Knock-knock!
Who's there?
Gumshoe.
Gumshoe who?
Gumshoe my house later and we'll play Fortnite!

Knock-knock!
Who's there?
Hay Man.
Hay Man who!
Hay Man, what's up?

Knock-knock!
Who's there?
Heidi.
Heidi who?
No, I'm not hiding, I'm standing right here!

Knock-knock!
Who's there?
Lace.
Lace who?
Lace who's on the head of those sharks, look out!

Knock-knock!
Who's there?
Onesie.
Onesie who?
Onesie your best friends!

Knock-knock!
Who's there?
Paradox
Paradox who?
Paradox here. We heard you were sick.

Knock-knock!
Who's there?
Plague.
Plague who?
Plague good game today!

Knock-knock!
Who's there?
Taro.
Taro who?
Terre Haute, Indiana? No, we're going to the Island.

Knock-knock!
Who's there?
Eon.
Eon who?
Eon who Reeves, star of *The Matrix*.

Knock-knock!
Who's there?
Fate.
Fate who?
Fate in your abilities will get you through this next battle.

Knock-knock!
Who's there?
Rex.
Rex who?
I'll Rex YOU!

Knock-knock!
Who's there?
Hime.
Hime who?
Hime here to see you!

Knock-knock!
Who's there?
Omega.
Omega who?
Omega you battle me right now!

Knock-knock!
Who's there?
Llama.
Llama who?
Llama be playing later, how about you?

Knock-knock!
Who's there?
Deep Fried.
Deep Fried.
It's not Deep Fried who, it's deep fried what!

Knock-knock.
Who's there?
Spears.
Spears who?
Spears the deal — it's our squad that's gonna win, or theirs!

Knock-knock!
Who's there?
ELIM
ELIM who?
NO, *I'm* ELIM.

Knock-knock!
Who's there?
Giddy Gunner.
Giddy Gunner who?
Giddy Gunner gonna getcha!

Knock-knock!
Who's there?
Bamboo.
Bamboo who?
There's no need to cry about it.

Knock-knock!
Who's there?
Gun.
Gun who?
[Silence]
What? Gun already?

Knock-knock!
Who's there?
Pickaxe.
Pickaxe who?
Pickaxe and get on with it!

Knock-knock!
Who's there?
Drumbeat.
Drumbeat who?
Drumbeat a lot of other objects in Fortnite!

Knock-knock!
Who's there?
Lucky.
Lucky who?
Lucky you!

Knock-knock!
Who's there?
A.X.E.
A.X.E. who?
A.X.E. me what?

Knock-knock!
Who's there?
Stop Axe.
Stop Axe who?
Stop Axe so many questions!

Knock-knock!
Who's there?
Warden.
Warden who?
Warden you like to know!

Knock-knock!
Who's there?
Ninja.
Ninja who? Hey, where did you go?

Knock-knock!
Who's there?
Best Mates!
Best Mates who?
Us, let's emote!

Knock-knock.
Who's there?
Boogie bomb.
Boogie bomb who?
BOOM!

Knock-knock.
Who's there?
Interrupting rifle.
Interrupting rifle wh--
Bang!

Knock-knock!
Who's there?
Mako.
Mako who?
Mako you take this glider.

Knock-knock!
Who's there?
Paradigm.
Paradigm who?
Paradigm out here on your porch.

Knock-knock!
Who's there?
Mushroom.
Mushroom who?
Mushroom to find healing items.

Knock-knock!
Who's there?
Giddy-Up.
Giddy-Up who?
Giddy-Up off your behind and let me in!

Knock-knock!
Who's there?
Guan Yu.
Guan Yu who?
Guan Yu start the game and I'll join you.

Knock-knock!
Who's there?
Bacon.
Bacon who?
Bacon some Energy Cells today!

Knock-knock!
Who's there?
Eternal.
Eternal who?
Eternally yours!

Knock-knock!
Who's there?
Broken Sword.
Broken Sword who?
Ah, it's pointless.

Knock-knock!
Who's there?
Guitar.
Guitar who?
Guitar weapons and go, boys!

●

Knock-knock!
Who's there?
Anita.
Anita who?
Anita use your AR!

●

Knock-knock!
Who's there?
Missile.
Missile who?
Missile you, haven't seen you in a while!

CHAPTER 9
WORDPLAY

Don't be a nerd, check out these words!

"I play Fortnite every seven days," said First Shot weakly.

•

"This chest is empty," Master Grenadier hollered.

•

"I think Bunny Brawler is adorable," Rabbit Raider said acutely.

•

"One more AR makes for 15 weapons," Burnout added.

•

"One more in the field makes 100!" Devastar admitted.

•

"Why don't you have some fruit?" Grimbles applied.

"The end of a game is overrated," said Jumpshot anticlimactically.

•

"I'm so glad I can play Fortnite on my MacBook," the player said applaudingly.

•

"This weapon is of greater value to you every day," appreciated Moniker.

•

"I'm a better shot than William Tell," said Assault Trooper arrowgantly.

•

"The roof of this structure about to collapse," Crimson Scout upheld.

•

"This chest is empty," said Brainiac vacuously.

•

"I came here via glider," said Liteshow, visibly moved.

"And this is a toilet seat I found in Flush Falls," Whiplash went on.

"I have the map memorized," Garrison wrote.

•

"This is just the big tool I need," said Rex with a heavy accent.

•

"Look, a Zapper!" Tinseltoes beamed.

•

"The Storm took Dominator!" said Grill Sergeant mistakenly.

•

"I will not finish in fifth place," the player held forth.

"Do I have time to go to the bathroom before the Battle Bus leaves?" Zenith prezoomed to ask.

●

"All I want is twenty thousand machine guns," said the player disarmingly.

●

"That bomb exploded so hard smoke is coming off of it," Warpaint fumed.

●

"Lobbers are coming, so I'm out of here," said the player believingly.

●

"Our maps of the island were stolen!" said Tracker xerographically.

●

"My weapon is dull," said Enforcer pointlessly.

●

"Argh, I've just been stabbed!" said Musha half-heartedly.

"Of course I can make armor out of chains," Oblivion replied by mail.

•

"I hate shellfish," said Leviathan crabbedly.

•

"Let's celebrate our victory," the player said, dancing around the issue.

"My chute weighs only two kilograms," said Lynx parametrically.

•

"I'll get you out of the prison in no time," said Glimmer balefully.

•

"Okay, you can borrow my AR again," Dire relented.

•

"The rules of the game say the building must go here," the player cited.

•

"I don't feel like dancing," Shogun said emotionally.

•

"That's the only way out over there!" Wukong pointed out.

•

"Can I use this sword?" Eon cut in sharply.

"It's better to loot together," Flytrap corroborated.

•

"Oops, I've ripped my pants!" was Chomp Sr.'s unseemly comment.

•

"The campfire's going out!" Calamity bellowed.

•

"I'm dying," Sun Strider croaked.

•

"I could use some goggles," Maximillian speculated.

•

"Let's walk quickly," said Sleuth stridently.

•

"That Husk seems to be rotting more than the last time I saw it," said Raven neurotically.

"I'm very powerful!" said Leviathan, superficially.

•

"I don't have any heavy bullets left," First Shot said lightly.

•

"Yes, I'm that strongly built," said Havoc soberly.

"This burger sure is hard to chew," Machinist beefed jerkily.

"I'm meeting a friend at Snobby Shores tonight," said Rabbit Raider sedately.

"I don't always lose Battle Royale, you know," the Fortnite player said winsomely.

TONGUE TWISTERS

Trees have thick trunks? Tut-tut! Chests are thick trunks.

You can wiggle, you can worm, but you can't do the wiggle worm.

Knock Knox? No, Ninja, no!

Bogey Bag Back Bling.

Are Mist Monsters Mythic?

•

The Flinger has no fingers, so why did you bring 'er?

•

I might like more Fortnite if I'm going to be forthright tonight.

•

Durrr Burger? Grr.

•

Risky Reels really reveals real regrets.

•

Moisty Merman met Maki Monster and made mincemeat out of mini marauders.

•

Let's loot Leaky Lake then take the loot to a loot llama at Lucky Landing.

Ladies love Lazy Links, but fellas are fond of Fatal Fields.

•

Dusty Divot dirty? Fah! It's full of flourishing fauna, friend!

•

Glimmer did the Shimmer, and shimmer did Glimmer.

•

Get green guns and get gray guns, Gus!

•

Build a big brick building.

•

What? A wall in Wailing Woods? Wow!

•

BRB! We need V-bucks!

•

Snobby Shores surely shows up Shifty Shafts.

The loneliest ledge in the lost Lonely Lodge.

•

There's a lot less love in Lonely Lodge than at Lazy Links lately.

RIDDLES

My name sounds like a word that means "Accidents," but if you come across me, the damage is no fluke.
Who am I?
Rex.

•

My name reminds you of oatmeal, but I'm much more devastating than that.
Who am I?
Musha.

•

That Marvel movie stole my name!
Who am I?
Ragnorok.

There is only one of me, but I am two.
Who am I?
Double Agent.

●

Let me get to the "point." I rock.
Who am I?
Power Chord.

If I'm the last one standing, it's because I shot last, pretty ironic considering my name.
Who am I?
First Shot.

•

I'm pink and fuzzy but I can hear you doubt me with my big ears.
Who am I?
Raider.

I'm not an artist, but I draw pretty well.
Who am I?
Quickdraw.

You'll suffer damage from me, but you should have seen that coming.
Who am I?
Energy Thief.

I can hold a ton of treasures, more than you ever would think possible. Don't leave me unattended or I'll go fast!
What am I?
A chest.

If you drop something, I'll probably grab it.
What Outlander am I?
Reclaimer.

Roses are red, apples are redder,
Most games are good, but Fortnite is better.

●

Roses are red,
You play Fortnite a lot,
You don't have a shield, and could sure use a pot.

●

Roses are red,
Fortnite's the best,
I got bit by a Mimic that I thought was a chest.

●

Roses are red,
Fortnite is easy,
A meal from Durrr Burger would be incredibly greasy.

●

Roses are red,
Weapons you tote.
If you do well in Fortnite, you get to emote.

Roses are red,
Victory's far,
Teammates are all gone, better pick up that SCAR.

BOOKS FOR FORTNITERS

Uncommon Eggs and Ham
Harold and the Epic Crayon
Anne of Uncommon Gables
One Fish, Two Fish, Red Fish, Rare Fish
The Mythic Compass
Trainee Fang
Island of the Rare Dolphins

There's one more fact we wanted to tell you about Fortnite. So we're leaving it right here. It's a Fortnote Footnite, no, wait, a Fortfoot Notenite. No, rather, a Fortnite Footnote. Yeah!

CHAPTER 10
ZANY!

Just some jokes that are zanier than a guy with a tomato head doing the Zany emote!

How can you tell if your best friend is a Fortnite fanatic?
They can't so much as finish their homework without doing a long, elaborate dance afterward.

How can you tell if *you're* a Fortnite fanatic?
When you put on clothes in the morning, you call it a "skin."

What's the difference between a neighborhood nuisance and a Fortnite scout?
One's a raccoon and the other does recon.

What do a door and a Fortnite noob have in common?
They both get knocked a lot.

What kind of pop should Fortniters never drink?
Shield pop!

Where do Fortniters sleep?
In a nite fort!

What's the healthiest part of a Fortnite character?
Their "heals."

What do Fortnite characters do on a launchpad?
They eat launch.

●

What's a Fortnite player's favorite kind of music?
Kinetic Beats!

●

Did you hear about the Fortnite fan too tired to play Fortnite?
She must have been hit by an Energy Thief.

●

What Fortnite mode do cows prefer?
Cattle Royale.

●

Why are skeletons terrible Fortnite players?
No skins!

●

But if they did play, who would they like best?
Bonesy.

What did the Recon Scout study in school?
Reconomics.

How is the Fortnite alphabet different from ours?
It only has 25 letters…somebody took the L.

Why is playing Fortnite like watching an *X-Men* movie?
You know eventually there will be a storm.

Why are Strikers no fun in Fortnite?
They never Battle Pass!

How can you tell someone is a Fortniter by looking at their feet?

They have extra heals.

●

What's a Fortniter's favorite Disney movie?

Snow White and the Seven Dwarf Husks.

●

How do Fortniters eat their soup?

They slurp it.

●

What's a good name for a Fortnite player?

Mat.

●

Why do Fortnite players totally rock?

Because their metal levels are very high.

●

Who's a Fortnite's favorite president?

Bush.

I think I've been playing too much Fortnite. I saw a stack of pallets the other day and I thought about smashing them. Wooden you?

●

Why is Fortnite better than a trip to Italy?
Because Fortnite has Tilted Towers and they've only got the one Leaning Tower.

●

What happens after you drink too much Slurp Juice?
You burp juice!

What NBA team do Fortniters root for?
Houston Rocket Riders

●

What other NBA team do Fortniters root for?
Milwaukee V-Bucks.

●

What baseball team do Fortniters love?
Kansas City Royales.

●

How do you make tea after a big Fortnite battle?
With Royaled water.

●

What's the soundtrack of Fortnite?
Rocket roll music.

●

Why are battles so much fun?
They're such a "rush"!

Why did the player just hang out and camp?
He needed to bush up on his survival skills.

•

Why couldn't the Fortniter grab a burger?
It wasn't his Durrrn.

•

PLAYER: Hey llama, you wanna come out and fight?
LLAMA: Sure, alpaca lunch.

•

Did you hear about the Fortnite playing dog?
He can heal on command!

Why does Batman hate Fortnite?
The Penguins.

•

What's another name for the Battle Bus?
Fortnite Mobile.

•

In Fortnite, they call Christmas Noe. Why?
Someone took the L.

•

What's a good name for the guy who takes you into battle?
Bus-Ter.

•

There's one Fortnite hero who's such a great friend, always
there to prop you up when you're feeling low. I guess
that's why they call him Support Specialist.

•

What did the two players on gliders say to each other?
"Hey, it's nice hanging out with you!"

What *should* B.A.S.E. stand for?
Blasts Are Severely Excruciating!

•

How is playing Fortnite like doing dishes at a restaurant?
A lot of bussing.

•

How does a Llama heal?
It eats a big bowl of llama beans.

•

**Did you know the pterodactyl glider releases water
without a trace?**
Sure, the P is silent.

•

If you build a castle and stay there for two weeks, you've
just had a fortnight in Fortnite.

•

What do you never want to taste in Fortnite?
A crescent . . . kick.

Shouldn't it be called a *Lloot* Llama?

●

What do Fortniters do in art class?
They don't draw or paint, but they do trace.

●

What's the most popular sport on the island?
Shield hockey.

●

What should you do if you're not going to play Fortnite for a while?
Leave a Fortnote.

●

It's not a real game of Fortnite unless you play it uninterrupted for two weeks.

●

Did you hear that Queen Elizabeth is into Fortnite?
Well, the Battle Royal version.

What's the most frightening thing on the news in Fortnite?

The weather report.

●

If a Fortniter working at a frozen yogurt shop could only keep one kind of yogurt — chocolate or whirled — which would she throw out?

She'd save the whirled!

●

What's the best day in Fortnite school?

The day they take a shield trip!

●

What did one squadmate say to the other who was knocked in the Storm?

"You're looking pretty under the weather."

●

What's the difference between your favorite game and a soccer match?

One is a Fortnite, and the other is a sport night.

What game do horses love?
Fortneight.

•

Last night I dreamt that the Fortnite servers were permanently down.
Talk about a Fortnitemare!

•

When you aren't sure if your parents will let you play, that's called a Fortmight.

•

Can you play Fortnite without a computer?
Sure, you can play Blanket Fortnite.

•

When's it time to eat in Fortnite?
When it's Forknite.

•

What will really bug you in Fortnite?
The Fort-mites.

What kind of shoes do Fortniters like best?
High heals.

Can you play Fortnite whenever you like?
Yeah, you've got the Fortright!

Did you hear about the Fortniter who earned bananas on his first try? It was . . . nuts.

Are there dogs in Fortnite?
Sure, hot dawgs!

●

What show do Fortniters never miss?
Outlander.

●

What's a Fortniter's favorite hockey team?
The New York Rangers.

●

What's a Fortniter's favorite football team?
The Minnesota Dark Vikings.

●

What's a good name for the pregame?
The calm before the storm.

●

Have you ever used the Banana emoji?
You should, he's very appealing.

What do you call a horse in Fortnite?
A Fortnite Mare.

How do Fortniters like their steak cooked?
Rare!

Who is a Fortniter's favorite superhero?
Iron Man.

How do you find metallic building materials in Fortnite?
Just steel them!

That Battle Royale round was boring . . . but then it really
ramped up!

What color does a Fortniter think grass is?
Uncommon!

What's a good name for a skilled looter?
Chester!

●

What do Bush Wookies eat?
Bush Wookie cookies!

●

What do flowers on the island do?
They BLOOOOOM!

●

What do you call a new Fortniter's screen?
The Noob Tube.

●

How do Fortniters groom themselves?
They bush their hair.

●

What happened to the sneaky sniper?
He bolted!

Look at this noob. What a no-skin!
No-skin! Aaaaaah!

•

What's a candy Fortniters like?
Tac-Tacs!

•

What day is it always for noobs?
Garbage Day.

•

What's a nice name for a great Fortnite player?
G.G.!

•

Are there armies in Fortnite?
Sure, they hold your gunsies!

•

**What's it called when you and your friend both want a
    rematch?**
A duo-ver!

What kind of hot dog is a Hot Dawg?
An Oscar Mire.

●

The only certainties in Fortnite are death and axes.

●

If it took four members of your squad an hour to build a wall, how long would it take another squad of six to build it?
No time at all — the wall is already built!

●

What cool animated cartoon character do Fortniters enjoy?
The Transcendent Panther!

●

What hospital show do Fortniters watch?
Uncommon Anatomy.

●

What kind of instrument does a Fortniter play?
The floot!

What kind of cereal does a Fortniter eat for breakfast?
Loot Loops!

•

What should the publisher of Fortnite be called?
Purple Games!

•

In Fortnite, it's never the end of the world…but it is
Llamageddon.

•

Remember: Sticks and stones may break your bones . . .
and so will Husks, other Mist Monsters, other players,
weapons . . .